Purpose and Hope with

God as your Captain

25 Days of Biblical Truths with My Prayers and Notes of Encouragement for *You*— an Amazing Young Man

Introduction

The waves of life can toss you around. Sometimes the future seems cloudy and you may not know which direction to turn. With God as the Captain of your life, you can have grounded confidence. He will direct your path and at the same time, bring clarity, purpose and meaning to your life. During the journey, His presence will guide you through storms, the Bible will help you to discern right from wrong to avoid disaster, and ultimately, with Christ as your hope, joyous Heaven awaits at the end.

This book was given to you from someone who really cares about you. Days 1-13 walks you through the gospel of Jesus Christ and what it means to be a Christian. Each day in this section, also includes a hymn of the Christian faith that expresses fundamental truths. Days 14-25 include other important topics which can foster deeper discussion with someone you trust. There are prayers and personalized notes throughout the book from the person who gave you this gift.

Current events can cause overwhelming fear and terror. There is chaos all around. In these uncertain times, there is no better comfort than the good news and hope of Jesus Christ and the security that can be found, when he is directing your course. I hope this book encourages you and impacts you life in a real and meaningful way.

May God bless you,

~Rebekah Tague

Daily Topics

Day 1- God's Greatness and Holiness

Day 2- Created by God

Day 3- The Devastation of Sin

Day 4- The Sacrifice of Love Jesus Made for You

Day 5- God's Gift of Salvation

Day 6- Understanding God's Grace and Forgiveness

Day 7- The Hope of Heaven

Day 8- The Joy in Christ's Return

Day 9- Your Heritage in Christ

Day 10- God is Your Refuge

Day 11- God is With You

Day 12- God has a Purpose for Your Life

Day 13- The Peace of Christ

Day 14- Healing in Mind, Body and Soul

Day 15- Christian Mentoring and Support

Day 16- Godly Family Role Models

Day 17- Characteristics of Safe People

Day 18- Good Friends

Day 19- A Wonderful Future Wife

Day 20- Discernment

Day 21- Healthy Boundaries

Day 22- Wisdom Beyond Measure

Day 23- A Godly Leader

Day 24- Talents and Abilities

Day 25- A Courageous Spirit

Day 1

God's Greatness and Holiness

Great:

CHIEF; OF VAST POWER AND EXCELLENCE; SUPREME; ILLUSTRIOUS; AS THE GREAT GOD; THE GREAT CREATOR

The Bible says...

For since the creation of the world His invisible attributes, His eternal power and divine nature, have been clearly seen, being understood through what has been made, so that they are without excuse.

ROMANS 1:20

We can learn about God and know that he is real by looking around at all he has made. Think about stars, your favorite animal or a beautiful place in nature. Aren't these wonderful? They all tell of God's greatness. There are many complex mysteries about God's creations that scientists have yet to understand.

Your, O Lord, is the greatness and the power and the glory and the victory and the majesty, indeed everything that is in heavens and the Earth, Yours is the dominion, O Lord, and You exalt Yourself as head over all.

1 CHRONICLES 29:11

God has always existed, even before he created the world. He is the author of time, the all powerful God who is to be revered and honored. He is in charge of all creation.

"HOLY, HOLY, HOLY is THE LORD GOD, THE ALMIGHTY, WHO WAS AND WHO IS AND WHO IS TO COME."
REVELATION 4:8

God resides in Heaven surrounded by angels and heavenly beings. He is the ruler of the entire universe. He is perfect and pure.

Bless the LORD, O my soul! O LORD my God, You are very great; You are clothed with splendor and majesty...
PSALM 104:1

God is glorious and full of splendor and majesty. He deserves honor and praise.

A prayer for you...

God, you are so excellent and great, you rule the universe with power and might. You set the world into motion. All creation tells of who you are and your everlasting greatness. Please help _____ to understand this and get a glimpse of how mighty and extraordinary you are.

Great is the Lord, His Power is Great

Great is the Lord, His power is great, my tongue His mighty acts relate:
Adore and fear the sovereign Lord, who rules all nature by His word.

He speaks—the gathering clouds obey; thick darkness veils the face of day;
Swift lightnings burst the pitchy cloud, and awful thunders roar aloud.

Roused at His call the winds awake, and from their wings destruction shake;
With groans the bending woods resound, and cast their honors to the ground.

On mounting waves the sailors rise, they seem to touch the very skies;
Instant they plunge with dreadful hiss, o'erwhelmed and lost in the abyss.

Well may poor mortals fear and quake, his voice makes hills and mountains shake:
Far o'er the land the billows dash, and cities fall with hideous crash.

He speaks—the winds their fury cease, the raging waves are hushed to peace,
Nature her calmest look puts on, well pleased the sudden night is gone.

Great is the Lord, His power is great, my tongue His mighty acts relate:
Adore and fear the sovereign Lord, who rules all nature by His word.

JOHN NEEDHAM, 1768

Nature speaks of God's greatness...

Day 2

You are Created by God

Create:

TO BEGET, TO GENERATE, TO BRING FORTH

The Bible says...

In the beginning God created the heavens and the earth.

Genesis 1:1

In the beginning, God started this world and created every living thing. He made the heavens and the earth. This same God created you.

I will give thanks to You, for I am fearfully and wonderfully made; wonderful are Your works, and my soul knows it very well.

Psalm 139:14

Everyone created by God is fearfully and wonderfully made and important to him.

For You formed my inward parts; you wove me in my mother's womb.

Psalm 139:13

God was making and creating you before you were even born! He saw you as he formed you.

The Spirit of God has made me, and the breath of the Almighty gives me life.

Job 33:4

God is the one who gives you life and breath. He has a plan for you.

God created man in His own image, in the image of God He created him; male and female He created them.
GENESIS 1:27

God made you so unique. You are unlike any other person that has ever lived. You are incredibly valuable to God because he made you by his own hand.

A prayer for you...

You, the Creator of the sky, the billions of stars, the moon and all of creation have made _____. Thank you God for making him. He is your amazing and complex creation. I am so glad that you care for him. May he understand his purpose and worth because he is handmade by you. Let him have a deep sense of value and belonging because you love him.

All Things Bright and Beautiful...

All things bright and beautiful, all creatures great and small,
All things wise and wonderful, the Lord God made them all.

Each little flow'r that opens, each little bird that sings,
He made their glowing colors, he made their tiny wings.

The purple-headed mountain, the river running by,
The sunset, and the morning that brightens up the sky.

The cold wind in the winter, the pleasant summer sun,
The ripe fruits in the garden, he made them, ev'ry one.

The tall trees in the greenwood, the meadows where we play,
The flowers by the water we gather ev'ry day.

He gave us eyes to see them, and lips that we might tell
How great is God Almighty, who has made all things well.

CECIL FRANCES ALEXANDER, 1848

God did an excellent job when he made you...

You are a priceless treasure of great worth. Your life matters!

Day 3

The Devastation of Sin

Sin:

To depart voluntarily from the path of duty prescribed by God to man; to violate the divine law in any particular, by actual transgression or by the neglect or non-observance of its injunctions…

The Bible says...

The Lord God gave the man [Adam] this order: You are free to eat from any of the trees of the garden except the tree of knowledge of good and evil. From that tree you shall not eat; when you eat from it you shall die.
GENESIS 2:16

He [the Devil as a snake] asked the woman [Eve], "Did God really say, 'You shall not eat from any of the trees in the garden'?"..."You certainly will not die!"
GENESIS 3:4

Satan, also known as the devil, was one of God's angels. He disobeyed God and now he is the enemy of God, trying to deceive and lie to people. Satan tempted the first man and woman, Adam and Eve, and they sinned by choosing to disobey God. As a result of this, sin entered the human heart and people and God are now separated because of sin.

Now the deeds of the flesh are evident, which are: immorality, impurity, sensuality, idolatry, sorcery, enmities, strife, jealousy, outbursts of anger, disputes, dissensions, factions, envying, drunkenness, carousing, and things like these...
GALATIANS 5:19-21

Sin is the opposite of what God wants. For example, God wants morality, kindness, purity, peace, soberness and love. Sin goes against all things good.

...for all have sinned and fall short of the glory of God...
ROMANS 3:23

Sins are the wrong things that we do. God is a pure and flawless being who can not tolerate sin. When we sin it hurts God deeply. Every person has sinned and gone against God's perfect will.

...the blazing furnace, where there will be weeping and gnashing of teeth.
MATTHEW 13:42

God lives in Heaven, a beautiful, joyful and amazing place. Because of sin, we are destined for an eternity separated from God. That miserable place is called hell. There is nothing good or cheerful in hell. The only thing that happens there is evil and terrible suffering with a complete absence from God's presence, goodness and glory.

A prayer for you...

God, sin separates us from you. Please help _____ to understand more about what sin is and how it hurts you. Help him to have a clear picture of the danger and horror of sin. Let him know that a world with sin is not what you intended or wanted when you made him, or your creation. Because of the evil in the human heart, we are separated from you God. Please help him to realize this.

Sin Can Never Enter There

Heaven is a holy place, filled with glory and with grace-
Sin can never enter there;
All within its gates are pure, from defilement kept secure-
Sin can never enter there.

Sin can never enter there, Sin can never enter there;
So if at the judgment bar sinful spots your soul shall mar,
You can never enter there.

If you hope to dwell at last, when your life on earth is past, in that home so bright and fair, you must here be cleansed from sin,
Have the life of Christ within- sin can never enter there.

You may live in sin below, Heaven's grace refuse to know,
But you cannot enter there; it will stop you at the door,
Bar you out forevermore- sin can never enter there.

If you cling to sin till death, when you draw your latest breath,
    You will sink in dark despair to the regions of the lost,
    Thus to prove at awful cost, sin can never enter there.

    Charles W. Naylor, 1899

Farewell to Sin.

I will part with thee, old master; this is my firm resolve;
And I'll boldly state my reason, why we must now dissolve.

The wages of sin is death, the wages of sin is death,
The wages of sin is death, and woe, and bitter remorse; I've found it so;
Bitter, bitter, bitter remorse and woe.

I have served thee [sin] long and faithful, confessed you were my lord;
All your way was dark and painful, and what is my reward?

I have given time and talents, my health and honor, too,
And exposed my soul to torments, and what did you bestow?

You have flattered me, and promised much pleasure in your reign;
I have sowed and reaped your harvest, now what my wretched gain?

While beneath your doleful bondage, how oft your father came,
Saying, "There is here no passage out from your dark domain."

But the blood of my Redeemer has saved me through and through,
So, in Jesus' name, forever I bid all sin adieu.

DANIEL S. WARNER, 1893

Day 4

The Sacrifice of Love Jesus Made for You

Sacrifice:

TO DESTROY, SURRENDER OR SUFFER TO BE LOST FOR THE SAKE OF OBTAINING SOMETHING

The Bible says...

You know that He appeared in order to take away sins; and in Him there is no sin.

1 JOHN 3:5

Jesus was perfect. He willingly came from Heaven to Earth as God's son. He lived as a man and never committed a single sin.

For God so loved the world, that He gave His only begotten Son, that whoever believes in Him shall not perish, but have eternal life.

JOHN 3:16

The punishment for sin is death and an eternity in hell away from God. God put all the punishment of sin, that should have been ours, on his precious and perfect son Jesus, whom he loved.

He [God] made Him [Jesus] who knew no sin to be sin on our behalf, so that we might become the righteousness of God in Him.

1 CORINTHIANS 5:21

God loves you so much that he sent Jesus, as a willing and perfect gift, to sacrifice his life for you.

But He was pierced through for our transgressions, He was crushed for our iniquities; The chastening for our well-being fell upon Him, and by His scourging we are healed.

Isaiah 53:5

All the punishment that we deserve was placed on Jesus. He paid the price that should have been ours. Because of this, there is a wonderful opportunity to have a relationship with God and to be close to God, just like God intended when he made the world.

A prayer for you...

Jesus, you loved us enough to willingly die on the cross for our sins. You took our punishment upon yourself. Please help _____ to know that you love him this deeply and that there is nothing he can do that will change the depth of your love for him.

Crucified for Me

Prince of glory condescended, He has favored me;
On the cross He meekly suffered my poor soul to free;
He has cleansed my inner being, changed my life of wrong;
How His touch of healing virtue fills my heart with song!

He was crucified for me, He was crucified for me, He was crucified for me,
On the cross of Calvary.

Oh, what consolation offered in His righteousness,
From the highest realm of glory coming down to this!
Here in gloomy maze He found me, languishing to die,
But the light from heaven streaming cleared my mortal sky.

When the pall of night was lifted hope began to start;
When the clouds so thick were rifted, light shone in my heart,
When the shock from Calv'ry's mountain shook my sinful soul,
Then the stream from that blest fountain over me did roll.

See the Sov'reign of creation, King of earth and skies,
All for sinful man's salvation thus He dies, He dies;
Yet He lives, a mighty Monarch, reigns o'er every foe,
Causing mortal man to triumph over sin below.

Barney E. Warren, 1900

Jesus gave his life for you. He loves you so much!

Day 5

The Gift of Salvation

Gift:

A PRESENT; ANY THING GIVEN OR BESTOWED; ANY THING, THE PROPERTY OF WHICH IS VOLUNTARILY TRANSFERRED BY ONE PERSON TO ANOTHER WITHOUT COMPENSATION

The Bible says...

He was buried, and...He was raised on the third day...
1 CORINTHIANS 15:4

Jesus died, but the wonderful news is that God is more powerful than death. Jesus conquered death and came back to life. He rose up to Heaven and now is seated next to God.

...that if you confess with your mouth Jesus as Lord, and believe in your heart that God raised Him from the dead, you will be saved...
ROMANS 10:9

If you choose to say that Jesus is Lord and put him in charge of your life, if you believe in your heart that Jesus died for your sins and rose up from the dead, then all your sins will be forgiven.

"Come now, and let us reason together," says the LORD, "Though your sins are as scarlet, they will be as white as snow; though they are red like crimson, they will be like wool..."
ISAIAH 1:18

God offers a free gift to you, which is complete forgiveness. If you accept Jesus and ask him to take charge of your life, your sins will be forgiven. This fixes the broken relationship between you and God. You can now be close to God and God views you as pure, holy and sinless because of what Jesus did for you.

"In the same way, I tell you, there is joy in the presence of the angels of God over one sinner who repents."

Luke 15:10

When we repent of our sins to God, acknowledge our wrongs and turn to Jesus, the angels in Heaven have great joy. They celebrate because the best decision was made. There is now life instead of death inside the person who asks God for help and forgiveness.

A prayer for you...

Please help _____ to understand what you did for him on the cross. Please work in his heart and life so that he can come to a decision to commit his life to you. Let him realize this free gift of salvation and a forever home in Heaven is nothing that can be earned.

It was Jesus Who Set Me Free

When I was treading the pathway of wrong,
When I was bound by the fetters so strong,
When I had lost all my sunshine and song, it was Jesus who set me free.

It was Jesus who set me free,
It was Jesus who set me free;
Now every chain has been broken in twain, it was Jesus who set me free.

When for my soul there was no one to care,
When condemnation seemed mine everywhere,
When I was bound by the chains of despair, it was Jesus who set me free.

When on my pathway no light seemed to shine, when I was dreading the judgment divine,
When evil powers seemed all to combine, it was Jesus who set me free.

When I am singing His glory and praise, marvelous, wonderful, infinite grace,
That He should suffer and die in my place- it was Jesus who set me free.

HALDOR LILLENAS, 1915

Day 6

God's Grace and Forgiveness

Grace:

THE FREE UNMERITED LOVE AND FAVOR OF GOD, THE SPRING AND SOURCE OF ALL THE BENEFITS MEN RECEIVE FROM HIM

The Bible says...

For as high as the heavens are above the earth, so great is His lovingkindness toward those who fear Him. As far as the east is from the west, so far has He removed our transgressions from us.

PSALM 103:11-12

Because of what Jesus did on the cross and because God loves us so much, there is complete forgiveness for every sin. God removes our sins. They are gone and no more.

He straightened up, and said to them, "He who is without sin among you, let him be the first to throw a stone at her." Again He stooped down and wrote on the ground. When they heard it, they began to go out one by one, beginning with the older ones, and He was left alone, and the woman, where she was, in the center of the court. Straightening up, Jesus said to her, "Woman, where are they? Did no one condemn you?" She said, "No one, Lord." And Jesus said, "I do not condemn you, either. Go. From now on sin no more.

JOHN 8:7-11

This is a perfect example of what Jesus does. He does not condemn us for our sins if we ask him to forgive us. He makes us clean and then we can have a new start to make better choices with his help.

But if it is by grace, it is no longer on the basis of works, otherwise grace is no longer grace.
ROMANS 11:6

God's grace and mercy can not be earned. You can not work to earn salvation, God's love or his favor. All of this has already been given to you by God out of his grace and mercy if you accept Jesus.

A prayer for you...

Thank you God for your forgiveness of sins and your grace. As _____ learns more about you, help him to understand that you care for him so much. Let him experience your grace and forgiveness in a deep and personal way. Help him to know your unconditional love for him.

Wonderful Grace of Jesus

Wonderful grace of Jesus, greater than all my sin;
How shall my tongue describe it, where shall its praise begin?
Taking away my burden, setting my spirit free;
For the wonderful grace of Jesus reaches me.

Wonderful the matchless grace of Jesus, deeper than the mighty rolling sea;
Higher than the mountain, sparkling like a fountain,
All-sufficient grace for even me!

Broader than the scope of my transgressions, greater far than all my sin and
Shame; oh, magnify the precious Name of Jesus, Praise His Name!
Wonderful grace of Jesus, reaching to all the lost,
By it I have been pardoned, saved to the uttermost;
Chains have been torn asunder, giving me liberty;
For the wonderful grace of Jesus reaches me.

Wonderful grace of Jesus, reaching the most defiled,
By its transforming power, making him God's dear child,
Purchasing peace and Heaven for all eternity-
And the wonderful grace of Jesus reaches me.

HALDOR LILLENAS, 1918

Come While He is Calling

If, dear sinner, you are longing all those sinful chains to break,
And relieve your soul from anguish, which no human form can take,
Then decide this very moment, that from bondage you'll be free;
Heed, oh, heed His wooing Spirit, come and He will pardon thee.

Then, oh, come while He is calling, lay your burden at His feet;
He will take away all anguish, if His promise you will meet.

Oh, dear sinner, do not tarry, when your soul in peril lies,
Though your sins be great like mountains, tow'ring upward to the skies;
For, from every one He'll free you, and a refuge He will be;
He's the blessed Rock of Ages that was cleft for you and me.

Turn, dear sinner, from the evils that have laden down your heart,
And have made your home unhappy- tis the demon's fiery dart;
Turn, oh, turn to Christ, our Savior, and for Him yield fruits of love,
Which will prove to all a blessing, and will crown your soul above.

NOAH H. BYRUM, 1897

God's forgiveness is wonderful!

Giving your life to Jesus is the best decision because...

_____
_____
_____
_____
_____
_____
_____
_____
_____
_____
_____
_____

How can someone become a Christian?

1) Understand that you have sinned and fallen short of God's glory.
...for all have sinned and fall short of the glory of God...Romans 3:23

2) Know that the wages of sin is an eternity of death.
For the wages of sin is death...Romans 6:23a

3) Understand that God gives you a free gift which is eternal life in Christ Jesus our Lord.
...but the free gift of God is eternal life in Christ Jesus our Lord...Romans 6:23b

4) Declare that Jesus is Lord and believe in your heart that God raised Him from the dead.
That if you confess with your mouth Jesus as Lord, and believe in your heart that God raised Him from the dead, you will be saved...Romans 10:9

A salvation prayer...

Dear Jesus, I am sorry for my sins. Thank you for taking my sins away by dying on the cross. I believe you were buried and then rose from the dead. I believe you returned to Heaven, and from there, you rule and reign. Please come into my life. I give you my life and surrender myself to you. Thank you that you love me and that I am now your child!

If you made the decision to follow Jesus...

Day 7

The Hope of Heaven

Hope:

CONFIDENCE IN A FUTURE EVENT; THE HIGHEST DEGREE OF WELL FOUNDED EXPECTATION OF GOOD; AS A HOPE FOUNDED ON GOD'S GRACIOUS PROMISES; A SCRIPTURAL SENSE

The Bible says...

...and He will wipe away every tear from their eyes; and there will no longer be any death; there will no longer be any mourning, or crying, or pain; the first things have passed away." And He [God] who sits on the throne said, "Behold, I am making all things new." And He said, "Write, for these words are faithful and true."

REVELATION 21: 4-5

The words of the LORD are pure words; as silver tried in a furnace on the earth, refined seven times.

PSALM 12:6

For those who make the decision to follow Jesus, there are some promises from God. God promises once in Heaven, he will wipe all tears from their eyes, there will be no more death, pain, sickness or suffering. When God says this, it is true because his words are pure and honest.

Death is swallowed up in victory. O death, where is your victory? O death, where is your sting?

1 CORINTHIANS 15:54-55

Death is all around us in this sin filled world. However, Jesus conquered and defeated death through his resurrection. After death, if we believe in Jesus, we immediately are welcomed into Heaven. God also promises that each of us will get a new eternal body, superior to this earthly body.

In My Father's house are many dwelling places; if it were not so, I would have told you; for I go to prepare a place for you. If I go and prepare a place for you, I will come again and receive you to Myself, that where I am, there you may be also.

JOHN 14:2-3

Heaven is a place where those who believe in Jesus will live. If you accept and believe the good news about what Jesus did, he will prepare a wonderful and special place in Heaven just for you. It will be perfect and stunning.

A prayer for you...

God, you live in Heaven, and it is more glorious than we can even imagine. It will be so spectacular, exciting and remarkable. There is pure joy and peace in Heaven, nothing painful, scary or evil. Death will be gone. Please help _____ to know that if he believes in you, he will live forever in Heaven with you.

Saint's Reward

Life on earth is but a vapor, soon we'll lay these bodies down;
But if we continue faithful, we shall wear the victor's crown-
Brighter than the stars of heaven, brighter than the dazzling sun,
We shall shine among the ransomed, when our work on earth is done.

We shall not abide forever in this gloomy vale of tears,
For our life shall, at the longest, only last a few short years;
Then we'll fly away to glory, at our Father's own right hand,
Help to sing redemption's story with the blood-washed angel band.

I would not give up my title to that future world of bliss
For the shining gold and silver of a thousand worlds like this;
I would rather bear affliction, be a hated pilgrim here,
Miss the diadems terrestrial, and obtain a crown up there.

Let us then be up and doing, we have but a few more days,
Priceless souls of men to rescue from their dark and sinful ways;
Courage, brother, work and suffer, till this fleeting life is past;
God will recompense our labors with a great reward at last.

WILLIAM G. SCHELL, 1900

Heaven is a place to look forward to!

Day 8

The Joy in Christ's Return

Return:

THE ACT OF COMING OR GOING BACK TO THE SAME PLACE

The Bible says...

But we do not want you to be uninformed, brethren, about those who are asleep, so that you will not grieve as do the rest who have no hope. For if we believe that Jesus died and rose again, even so God will bring with Him those who have fallen asleep in Jesus. For this we say to you by the word of the Lord, that we who are alive and remain until the coming of the Lord, will not precede those who have fallen asleep. For the Lord Himself will descend from Heaven with a shout, with the voice of the archangel and with the trumpet of God, and the dead in Christ will rise first. Then we who are alive and remain will be caught up together with them in the clouds to meet the Lord in the air, and so we shall always be with the Lord. Therefore comfort one another with these words.

1 Thessalonians 4:13-18

Just as Jesus went back up to Heaven after he rose from the grave, he is going to come back to Earth. He is going to retrieve all those who belong to him. This is comforting, because this life is just temporary and short compared to our eternal life, with Jesus, in Heaven.

For the grace of God has appeared, bringing salvation to all men, instructing us to deny ungodliness and worldly desires and to live sensibly, righteously and godly in the present age, looking for the blessed hope and the appearing of the glory of our great God and Savior, Christ Jesus, who gave Himself for us to redeem us from every lawless deed, and to purify for Himself a people for His own possession, zealous for good deeds.

TITUS 2:11-14

Living for Jesus and honoring him with your life is the best way to prepare for his approaching return.

Behold, I tell you a mystery; we will not all sleep, but we will all be changed, in a moment, in the twinkling of an eye, at the last trumpet; for the trumpet will sound, and the dead will be raised imperishable, and we will be changed. For this perishable must put on the imperishable, and this mortal must put on immortality.

1 CORINTHIANS 15:51-53

When Jesus returns, our bodies will change. We will have wonderful bodies with no illnesses or problems. We will have bodies that last forever.

But of that day and hour no one knows…For this reason you also must be ready; for the Son of Man is coming at an hour when you do not think He will.

Matthew 24:36 and 44

No one knows when Jesus will return. It is important to make the critical decision to follow him now before it is too late.

A prayer for you...

Lord, please work in _____'s life. Let him know that you are real and that you will be coming back one day. You may come back within his lifetime. Please help him to commit himself to you. Let him know what joy and gladness there will be when you return, for those who love you. It will be a long awaited, very exciting and glorious day.

We Know Not the Hour

We know not the hour of the Master's appearing, yet signs all foretell that the moment is nearing. When He shall return-'tis a promise most cheering- but we know not the hour.

He will come, let us watch and be ready; He will come, hallelujah! Hallelujah! He will come in the clouds of His Father's bright glory- but we know not the hour.

There's light for the wise who are seeking salvation, there's truth in the Book of divine revelation- each prophecy points to the great consummation- but we know not the hour.

We'll watch and we'll pray, with our lamps trimmed and burning, we'll work and we'll wait till the Master's returning, we'll sing and rejoice, every omen discerning- but we know not the hour.

Franklin E. Belden, 1886

Day 9

Your Heritage in Christ

Heritage:

THE SAINTS OR PEOPLE OF GOD ARE CALLED HIS HERITAGE AS BEING CLAIMED BY HIM, AND THE OBJECTS OF HIS SPECIAL CARE

The Bible says...

But you are a chosen people, a royal priesthood, a holy nation, a people for God's own possession, so that you may proclaim the excellencies of Him who has called you out of darkness into His marvelous light; for you once were not a people, but now you are the people of God; you had not received mercy, but now you have received mercy.

1 PETER 2:9

If you accept Jesus, you become royal and set apart. You are his child, rescued and called away from sin and darkness. You are now safe in God's merciful arms.

"And I will be a father to you, and you shall be sons and daughters to Me,"
says the Lord Almighty.

2 CORINTHIANS 6:18

If you commit your life to Jesus, you become God's precious child. You belong to him and now have the status as the son of the Almighty God! He gave his life so that you could be his.

If you then, being evil, know how to give good gifts to your children, how much more will your Father who is in Heaven give what is good to those who ask Him!
MATTHEW 7:11

Earthly fathers and mothers can fail miserably but God is your perfect and good Father in Heaven. He will watch over you, take care of you and give you his pure and unconditional love.

See how great a love the Father has bestowed on us, that we would be called children of God; and such we are. For this reason the world does not know us, because it did not know Him.
1 JOHN 3:1

God's love is so great for you that he was willing to die. He longs to call you his child and make you his own.

A prayer for you...

Thank you that _____ is someone you love so deeply. Thank you that he is (or can be) your child. Thank you for letting him come into my life. Help me to point him toward you, his loving and good Father. Lead him to realize that a rich and beautiful inheritance can be his if he has Christ. He is a prince, a royal young man in your eyes Jesus.

Because He Loves Me...

When the storm winds rage, and the rain falls fast, and the clouds hang low
above, I shall be secure till the storm is past, for I trust my Savior's love.
And He knows the way, and He holds my hand, and He will not let it go;
He will lead me home to that better land, just because He loves me so.

It was not that I was so good or great, for my heart was vile with sin;
I had turned my back on the narrow gate, neither care nor lived for Him,
But I pleased myself, and I chose my way, for His grace I did not know;
But He sought me still through the night and day, just because He loved me so.

If He loved me so when I grieved Him sore that He sought me tenderly,
Till He won my heart, and my sins He bore, so that I His child might be,
Will He love me less since I love Him, too, so my heart with fervor glows?
And I haste each day all His will to do that my willing spirit knows.

I will trust His love, for it e'er will last, it is rich and warm and free;
Through the years of life it will hold me fast, and my help and comfort be;
To my waiting heart all its treasures rare as a sparkling stream shall flow;
In the joy of God I shall ever share, just because He loves me so.

CHARLES W. NAYLOR, 1917

Day 10

God is Your Refuge

Refuge:

THAT WHICH SHELTERS OR PROTECTS FROM DANGER, DISTRESS OR CALAMITY; A STRONG HOLD WHICH PROTECTS BY ITS STRENGTH, OR A SANCTUARY WHICH SECURES SAFETY BY ITS SACREDNESS; ANY PLACE INACCESSIBLE TO AN ENEMY.

The Bible says...

God is our refuge and strength, a very present help in trouble. Therefore we will not fear, though the earth should change and though the mountains slip into the heart of the sea; Though its waters roar and foam, though the mountains quake at its swelling pride.

Psalm 46:1-3

God is right there with you in the midst of trouble. He is holding your hand and standing by you. He can be your source of strength when you feel like you have nothing left. He can be the one you turn to when the world around you is crashing down in chaos. Nothing is too great for him. For those who belong to Jesus, no trouble can separate them from the love and grace of God, or steal from them the promise of a secure eternity in heaven.

The Lord is my rock and my fortress and my deliver, My God, my rock, in whom I take refuge; my shield and the horn of my salvation, my stronghold.

Psalm 18:2

Sometimes you may feel like there is no one to run to. You may feel trapped as if the ground is falling from under your feet. God can hold you up and deliver you from evil.

The name of the Lord is a strong tower; the righteous run into it and are safe.
PROVERBS 18:10

When you feel scared and alone, cry out to Jesus because he will help you. Call to him and you will feel his presence and his protection.

The Lord also will be a stronghold for the oppressed, a stronghold in times of trouble, and those who know Your name will put their trust in You, for You, O Lord, have not forsaken those who seek You.
PSALM 9:9-10

When you feel oppressed and when you are struggling, that is when God shows up. If you know him and put your trust in him, he will work in some miraculous and unexpected ways. God will not forsake those who belong to him.

A prayer for you...

Lord, help _____ to know that he can turn to you and run toward you when he needs help. You are right by his side, ready to be his source of strength. Show him how you are safe, good and reliable.

Within the Rock

I have a sure and safe retreat to which I always flee,
from every storm of life I meet- tis Christ the Rock for me.

Within the Rock I safely hide, a glorious place for me;
There's naught more sure that can abide through time or eternity.

Though tempests rage and wild winds blow, whom can I trust but Thee?
I feel secure from every foe in Christ, the Rock for me.

Come stormy wind and rolling sea, come fire and tempest shock,
I'm in that cleft once made for me in Christ the solid Rock.

BARNEY E. WARREN, 1900

No matter what, you can take refuge in Jesus...

Day 11

God is With You

With:

In company

The Bible says...

But the Lord is faithful, and He will strengthen and protect you from the evil one.

2 THESSALONIANS 3:3

When we belong to Jesus, we can trust that God will give us strength in any situation. He will be our protector and defender from Satan. He is actively guarding and shielding those who belong to him.

The Lord is my shepherd, I shall not want. He makes me lie down in green pastures; He leads me beside quiet waters. He restores my soul; He guides me in the paths of righteousness for His name's sake. Even though I walk through the valley of the shadow of death, I fear no evil, for You are with me; your rod and Your staff, they comfort me. You prepare a table before me in the presence of my enemies; You have anointed my head with oil; my cup overflows. Surely goodness and lovingkindness will follow me all the days of my life, and I will dwell in the house of the Lord forever.

PSALM 23:1-6

Just as a shepherd watches over and cares for sheep, God is watching over you. He brings good things into your life. He is there in scary times, walking right beside you. He is there when you are surrounded by enemies. He promises that those who love him will spend eternity in Heaven with him.

You have enclosed me behind and before, and laid Your hand upon me.
PSALM 139:5

God goes ahead of you and behind you. He has been there in the hardest of times and already knows what your future holds. He is with you now. His hand is upon you. He is guiding you and leading you. He has good plans for you. His presence is surrounding you.

I will ask the Father, and He will give you another Helper, that He may be with you forever;
JOHN 14:16

Jesus promises the Holy Spirit, who is our Helper and advocate. He is there to comfort and give discretion. He is with those who believe.

A prayer for you...

Please help _____ to experience the reality of your presence in his life. Help him to know you are right there by him this very day. You see his situation and you are going to walk with him through every trial. You can be his strength, help, protector and guide if he calls out to you.

My Father Watches Over Me

I trust in God wherever I may be, upon the land, or on the rolling sea,
For come what may, from day to day, my heav'nly Father watches over me.

I trust in God, I know He cares for me; on mountain bleak or on the stormy sea;
Though billows roll, He keeps my soul; my heav'nly Father watches over me.

He makes the rose an object of His care, He guides the eagle through the pathless air, and surely He remembers me; my heav'nly Father watches over me.

I trust in God, for, in the lion's den, on battlefield, or in the prison pen, Through praise or blame, through flood or flame, my heav'nly Father watches over me.

The valley may be dark, the shadows deep, but, oh, the Shepherd guards His lonely sheep; and through the gloom He'll lead me home, My heav'nly Father watches over me.

WILLIAM C. MARTIN, 1910

When you feel alone, God is close by...

Day 12

God Has a Purpose for Your Life

Purpose:

To intend; to design; to resolve; to determine on some end or object to be accomplished

The Bible says...

Your [God's] eyes have seen my unformed substance; and in Your book were all written the days that were ordained for me, when as yet there was not one of them. How precious also are Your thoughts to me, O God! How vast is the sum of them! If I should count them, they would outnumber the sand...

Psalm 139:16-18

God knew you before you were born. He knew everything about you, how long you will live and what you will become. He thinks about you and cares for you so much, that all his thoughts for you outnumber the grains of sand!

And we know that God causes all things to work together for good to those who love God, to those who are called according to His purpose.

Romans 8:28

For the person who has committed their life to Jesus, God will work in their life. He has a purpose and a plan. He will take every situation, every difficult trial, and turn these around into something that will work for your good.

To comfort all who mourn, to grant those who mourn in Zion, giving them a garland instead of ashes, the oil of gladness instead of mourning, the mantle of praise instead of a spirit of fainting. So they will be called oaks of righteousness, the planting of the Lord, that He may be glorified.

ISAIAH 61:1-3

God can take the brokenness in your life, the lost hope, the hurt and the ashes of pain and disappointment and turn these into something beautiful. He can work in your life and turn your sorrow into joy. He can firmly establish you as a righteous strong pillar of strength. God is glorious and is able to do the impossible if you invite him to work in your life.

A prayer for you...

Thank you God that you have good plans for _____. You knew him since before he was born. You know the hurt and pain he has experienced. Please Lord, work in his life in anything, big or small, that he is facing right now. Help him to become all you have planned for him to be. Work through each circumstance in his life to fulfill your purpose for him.

God's Way is Best

God's way is best; if human wisdom a fairer way may seem to show,
It's only that our earth-dimmed vision the truth can never clearly know.

God's way is best, I will not murmur, although the end I may not see;
Where'er He leads I'll meekly follow, God's way is best, is best for me.

Had I the choosing of my pathway, in blindness I should go astray,
And wander far away in darkness, nor reach that land of endless day.

He leadeth true; I will not question, though through the valley I shall go;
Though I should pass through clouds of trial, and drink the cup of human woe.

God's way is best; heart, cease thy struggling to see and know and understand;
Forsake thy fears and doubts, but trusting, submit thyself into His hand.

Thy way is best, so lead me onward, my all I give to Thy control;
Thy loving hand will truly guide me, and safe to glory bring my soul.

CHARLES W. NAYLOR, 1904

God has a good plan and an important purpose for your life...

Day 13

The Peace of Christ

Peace:

FREEDOM FROM AGITATION OR DISTURBANCE…AS FROM FEAR, TERROR, ANGER, ANXIETY OR THE LIKE; QUIETNESS OF MIND; TRANQUILITY; CALMNESS; QUIET OF CONSCIENCE

The Bible says...

Be anxious for nothing, but in everything by prayer and supplication with thanksgiving let your requests be made known to God. And the peace of God, which surpasses all comprehension, will guard your hearts and your minds in Christ Jesus.
PHILIPPIANS 4:6-7

In some circumstances it is very easy to be anxious. You can take every situation that concerns you to Jesus. He will hear your prayers. He can flood your heart and mind with his peace, quiet your soul and provide you with rest.

...cast all your anxiety on Him, because He cares for you.
1 Peter 5:7

God is able to take all our worries and burdens upon himself. He cares for you so much. He is actively working in your life.

"Come to Me, all who are weary and heavy-laden, and I will give you rest. Take My yoke upon you and learn from Me, for I am gentle and humble in heart, and you will find rest for your souls. For My yoke is easy and My burden is light."
MATTHEW 11:28-30

Jesus says he will give rest to those who commit their lives to him. If you submit to Jesus, he will gently lead you to places of rest for your soul and mind.

These things I have spoken to you, so that in Me you may have peace. In the world you have tribulation, but take courage; I have overcome the world."

JOHN 16:33

Jesus tells us that even in trials, he can provide us with peace and courage. Jesus has overcome death and evil by dying on the cross and rising again. Because of this victory, we can have the ultimate peace, rest, and comfort for our soul.

A prayer for you...

Jesus, please give _____ your peace. Fill his heart with your comfort and love. Let him know you are watching over him. Show him that he can call out to you in any situation and share all his worries with you. In return, he can rest knowing that you are going to take care of him and guide him in the right way.

Prince of Peace Control My Will

Prince of peace, control my will,
Bid the struggling heart be still;
Bid my fears and doubtings cease,
Hush my spirit into peace.
Thou hast bought me with Thy blood,
Opened wide the gate to God;
Peace I ask- but peace must be,
Lord, in being one with Thee.
May Thy will, not mine, be done,
May Thy will and mine be one;
Chase these doubtings from my heart,
Now Thy perfect peace impart.
Savior, at Thy feet I fall,
Thou my life, my God, my all!
Let Thy happy servant be
One forevermore with Thee!

MARY A. S. BARBER, 1839

Day 14

Wellness in Mind, Body and Soul

Well:

BEING IN HEALTH; HAVING A SOUND BODY

The Bible says...

He heals the brokenhearted and binds up their wounds.
PSALM 147:3

God sees all your hurts and pain. He can bring healing and restoration to your spirit. It may not happen instantly, but he can make you whole and complete.

So I will restore to you the years that the swarming locust has eaten...
JOEL 2:25

God can take wasted years and those parts of life that seem to have been destroyed and lost, and completely reconstruct and fix all that was broken for his glory.

The Lord is near to the brokenhearted and saves those who are crushed in spirit.
PSALM 34:18

When you feel brokenhearted and hurt, when your spirit is crushed, God is near in that time. He will come and save you if you call out to him.

Is anyone among you sick? Then he must call for the elders of the church and they are to pray over him, anointing him with oil in the name of the Lord…
JAMES 5:14

If you are experiencing any type of sickness or emotional pain, there are people that can pray for you. It may not always be God's will to bring immediate healing, however sometimes he does choose and is able to heal in miraculous ways.

'Do not fear, for I am with you; do not anxiously look about you, for I am your God. I will strengthen you, surely I will help you, surely I will uphold you with My righteous right hand.'
ISAIAH 41:10

When you feel worried about emotional or physical health problems, God is right there with you to strengthen and help you. He will uphold you with his hand.

A prayer for you…

Thank you that when we get to Heaven there will not be a trace of emotional or physical pain. I pray for _____, that you will bring emotional healing in any area that he needs and restful peace to his spirit. Please work in his life to bring health to his body as well. Father, protect him and bless him in every way.

Resources for emotional healing include: the Bible, Christian therapists, trustworthy godly people and more...

Day 15

Christian Mentoring and Support

Mentor:

TO INSTRUCT; TO INFORM; TO COMMUNICATE TO ANOTHER THE KNOWLEDGE OF THAT WHICH HE WAS BEFORE IGNORANT

The Bible says...

I thank God, whom I serve with a clear conscience the way my forefathers did, as I constantly remember you in my prayers night and day...
2 TIMOTHY 1:3-4

I am praying for you and I am here to support you. You can share your prayer requests with me and I will remember you in prayer.

Be imitators of me, just as I also am of Christ.
1 CORINTHIANS 11:1

I am praying that there will be people that come into your life that represent Jesus well. Such people are genuine and trustworthy examples to learn from and follow. They are not hypocrites or abusers of the Christian faith.

A wise man will hear and increase in learning, and a man of understanding will acquire wise counsel...
PROVERBS 1:5

I am also praying that there will be wise people in your life. Listening to the wisdom of people who are older and strong in their walk with Jesus is so beneficial. You can gain from their wisdom and potentially spare yourself from problems.

Remember those who led you, who spoke the word of God to you; and considering the result of their conduct, imitate their faith.
Hebrews 13:7

People who are actively doing what the Bible (God's Word) says, are great examples to follow. If a person speaks truthfully about what the Bible says and then also acts in a way that pleases God, then that is the type of person that you want to learn from.

But the fruit of the Spirit is love, joy, peace, patience, kindness, goodness, faithfulness, gentleness, self-control; against such things there is no law.
Galatians 5:22-23

This is an example of what a follower of Christ should look like. As the Holy Spirit works in a person's life, they become more and more like how God wants them to be. A person who displays these traits would be a great example of a mentor and friend.

Please protect _____ from anyone that would want to pretend they are a Christian yet do him harm. Lord, please bring godly and kind people into his life that can encourage and support him in the ways that he needs. Please bring healthy role models as well. I pray that you will arrange circumstances where he will have such people in every season of his life.

I am here for you...

Day 16

Godly Family Role Models

Godly:

Living in obedience to God's commands, from a principle of love to him and reverence of his character and precepts

The Bible says...

Husbands, love your wives and do not be embittered [or harsh] against them.
COLOSSIANS 3:19

God desires and intends for a husband and wife to love each other. To treat one another with respect and kindness.

An overseer, then, must be above reproach, the husband of one wife, temperate, prudent, respectable, hospitable, able to teach, not addicted to wine or pugnacious, but gentle, peaceable, free from the love of money...
1 TIMOTHY 3:2-7

This is an example of what a godly man looks like. He is gentle, peaceful, loving and respectable. He takes care of his children and wife. His family loves him and others view him as a person of integrity.

Fathers, do not provoke your children to anger, but bring them up in the discipline and instruction of the Lord.
EPHESIANS 6:4

A father that is following Jesus will not purposely anger his children but he protects them and sets boundaries in a loving way to keep them safe. He teaches his children about Jesus.

She opens her mouth in wisdom, and the teaching of kindness is on her tongue. She looks well to the ways of her household, and does not eat the bread of idleness. Her children rise up and bless her; her husband also, and he praises her...Charm is deceitful and beauty is vain, but a woman who fears the Lord, she shall be praised.

Proverbs 31:26-30

A godly mother is kind. She looks after her children and cares for her family. She honors God and her family loves her.

Children, obey your parents in the Lord, for this is right.

Ephesians 6:1

In a family that lives for Jesus, children are commanded to obey and honor their parents. Now, if their parents are hurting them or behaving abusively, a child is not expected to obey their parents wishes. The parents are sinning against the child, this is evil and completely against what God wants.

A prayer for you...

God, thank you for the scripture examples of good family role models. Please bring godly family role models into _____'s life. Help him to be able to form good relationships with these people. No family is perfect and everyone needs your help to act in a way that honors you, but please surround him with families that love you God and want to please you with their actions.

Day 17

Characteristics of Safe People

Safe:

FREE FROM DANGER OF ANY KIND

The Bible says...

For men will be lovers of self, lovers of money, boastful, arrogant, revilers, disobedient to parents, ungrateful, unholy, unloving, irreconcilable, malicious gossips, without self-control, brutal, haters of good, treacherous, reckless, conceited, lovers of pleasure rather than lovers of God, holding to a form of godliness, although they have denied its power; Avoid such men as these.
2 TIMOTHY 3:2-5

All these examples describe unsafe people. People like this are not walking with God. They are not trustworthy or honorable.

Treat others the same way you want them to treat you.
NEHEMIAH 7:2

A safe person treats other people with respect and kindness.

Finally, brethren, whatever is true, whatever is honorable, whatever is right, whatever is pure, whatever is lovely, whatever is of good repute, if there is any excellence and if anything worthy of praise, dwell on these things.
PHILIPPIANS 4:8

People who love Jesus seek his help to set their minds on honorable things. They try to focus on true, moral, right, pure and lovely thoughts.

How can a young man (or woman) keep his way pure? By keeping it according to Your word.
PSALM 119:9

A safe person strives to honor God in purity. They want to please God with what they look at and listen to. They treat others with respect and purity.

So, as those who have been chosen of God, holy and beloved, put on a heart of compassion, kindness, humility, gentleness and patience…
COLOSSIANS 3:12

A safe person wants to honor God with their heart.

Do nothing from selfishness or empty conceit, but with humility of mind regard one another as more important than yourselves; do not merely look out for your own personal interests, but also for the interests of others.
PHILIPPIANS 2:3-4

A safe person considers others interests instead of just their own.

A prayer for you…

God please help _____ to learn what a safe person looks like and help him to seek out relationships with safe people. Bring these people into his life. Help him to grow into all you have planned.

Examples of trustworthy safe people...

Day 18

Good Friends

Friend:

ONE WHO IS ATTACHED TO ANOTHER BY AFFECTION; ONE WHO ENTERTAINS FOR ANOTHER SENTIMENTS OF ESTEEM, RESPECT AND AFFECTION WHICH LEAD HIM TO DESIRE HIS COMPANY AND TO SEEK TO PROMOTE HIS HAPPINESS AND PROSPERITY

The Bible says...

Do not be deceived: "Bad company corrupts good morals."
1 CORINTHIANS 15:33

Surrounding yourself with people who love God is important. Friends that are unhealthy will only bring you down and impact your life in a negative way.

Two are better than one because they have a good return for their labor. For if either of them falls, the one will lift up his companion. But woe to the one who falls when there is not another to lift him up.
ECCLESIASTES 4:9-10

A good friend will be there in times of trouble. They will help and encourage you toward the Lord.

The righteous is a guide to his neighbor, but the way of the wicked leads them astray.
PROVERBS 12:26

A good friend will give beneficial advice. They would not encourage you to engage in self destructive behaviors.

He who walks with wise men will be wise, but the companion of fools will suffer harm.
PROVERBS 13:20

Foolish people bring about harm. They do not think about their behaviors or future. Wise friends consider their actions and seek the Lord for guidance.

A friend loves at all times...
PROVERB 17:17

A good friend genuinely loves and cares about you. They listen to your concerns and are there for you through good and bad circumstances.

A prayer for you...

Please guide _____ through the process of finding good friends. Help him to be discerning. Protect him from bad company. Please lead him to quality friendships and guard him from dangerous relationships. Let him have at least one good friend through all the seasons of his life. Surround him with people that love you and care about him Lord.

Thoughts about how to choose a good friend...

Day 18

A Wonderful Future Wife

Future:

TIME TO COME; A TIME SUBSEQUENT TO THE PRESENT

The Bible says...

Do not be bound together with unbelievers, for what partnership have righteousness and lawlessness; or what fellowship has light with darkness?
1 CORINTHIANS 6:14

The Bible makes it clear about the importance of marrying a woman who is also a Christian. In this way, both the husband and wife have the same mindset. They are submitting to Jesus and loving each other with the strength of the Lord.

Therefore a man shall leave his father and his mother and hold fast to his wife, and they shall become one flesh.
GENESIS 2:24

In a Christian marriage, the man is to commit to his wife. He is to put his wife and children before others.

Husbands, love your wives, just as Christ also loved the church and gave Himself up for her...
EPHESIANS 5:25

A godly husband is a loving, caring and devoted man that will protect and sacrifice for his wife, just as Jesus sacrificed for us.

But seek first His kingdom and His righteousness, and all these things will be added to you.
MATTHEW 6:33

Seeking the Lord first and following him is the most valuable decision you can make. Ask for his help and provision for a wife. It may not come right away, but if it is God's will, he will bring a wife in his perfect timing.

Every good thing given and every perfect gift is from above, coming down from the Father of lights, with whom there is no variation or shifting shadow.
James 1:17

Every good thing is from God. Every wonderful gift, including a godly wife, is from him.

A prayer for you...

Lord, you know the future and _____ is in your hands. If it is in your will, please bring him a wonderful wife in your time. Help her to be a woman who loves you and honors and respects him. In the mean time, help him to grow close to you and surround himself with people that love you. Thank you God that you are holding his future and that you have great plans for him if he chooses to walk with you.

Good qualities to look for in a wife...

Day 20

Discernment

Discernment:

THE POWER OR FACULTY OF THE MIND, BY WHICH IT DISTINGUISHES ONE THING FROM ANOTHER, AS TRUTH FROM FALSEHOOD, VIRTUE FROM VICE

The Bible says...

And do not be conformed to this world, but be transformed by the renewing of your mind, so that you may prove what the will of God is, that which is good and acceptable and perfect.
ROMANS 12:2

In order to discern God's will, it is important to ask him to transform your mind and heart. When you ask God for help and direction and seek his will, you can clearly discern right from wrong.

Woe to those who call evil good, and good evil; who substitute darkness for light and light for darkness; who substitute bitter for sweet and sweet for bitter! Woe to those who are wise in their own eyes and clever in their own sight! Woe to those who are heroes in drinking wine and valiant men in mixing strong drink...
ISAIAH 5:20-22

Sometimes people will teach beliefs that sound good, but what they are saying is really evil and wrong. When reading the Bible and learning God's truth, the Holy Spirit can help you see through the lies of deceitful philosophies.

.....there are some who are disturbing you and want to distort the gospel of Christ. But even if we, or an angel from Heaven, should preach to you a gospel contrary to what we have preached to you, he is to be accursed!
GALATIANS 1:6-8

As a result, we are no longer to be children, tossed here and there by waves and carried about by every wind of doctrine, by the trickery of men, by craftiness in deceitful scheming...
EPHESIANS 4:14

These verses show that there are many people preaching false truths that are not Biblical. It is important to make sure that what a pastor says, matches with God's word.

And do not get drunk with wine, for that is dissipation, but be filled with the Spirit...
EPHESIANS 5:18

It is important to stay away from substances that will distort and impair your thinking and limit your ability to discern.

Do not judge according to appearance, but judge with righteous judgment.
JOHN 7:24

It is easy to judge someone by their appearance, but this is superficial and can be deceiving. Judging by a person's character and asking God for wisdom is the best way to discern.

A prayer for you...

Lord, please give _____ your wisdom and discernment. There are so many deceitful teachings that go against your word. Help him to know what is right and wrong. Also, please help him to avoid anything that would impair his thinking and ability to discern so that he can have soundness of mind and clarity in all situations.

Situations where discernment is important...

_____

_____

_____

_____

_____

_____

_____

Day 21

Healthy Boundaries

Healthy:

CONDUCIVE TO HEALTH; WHOLESOME; SALUBRIOUS

The Bible Says...

By the seventh day God completed His work which He had done, and He rested on the seventh day from all His work which He had done. Then God blessed the seventh day and sanctified it, because in it He rested from all His work which God had created and made.
GENESIS 2:2-3

God set an example by resting and we should too. Continually working and over committing without resting is stressful. It is important to set boundaries and say "no" when you feel overwhelmed.

Go to the ant...observe her ways and be wise...
PROVERBS 14:23

Setting boundaries with activities that are not beneficial and that steal your time and energy is necessary. Cutting things out of your life that waste your time will help you be more successful as you focus on what is important.

...not forsaking our own assembling together, as is the habit of some, but encouraging one another; and all the more as you see the day drawing near.
HEBREWS 10:25

Setting aside time to attend church and gather with other Christians is essential. Making this a priority is honoring to God.

And just as they did not see fit to acknowledge God any longer, God gave them over to a depraved mind, to do those things which are not proper, being filled with all unrighteousness, wickedness, greed, evil; full of envy, murder, strife, deceit, malice; they are gossips, slanderers, haters of God, insolent, arrogant, boastful, inventors of evil, disobedient to parents, without understanding, untrustworthy, unloving, unmerciful...

ROMANS 1:28-31

Setting boundaries with unhealthy people is necessary for your own personal safety and emotional well being. Avoid or limit contact with those who hurt you, make you feel bad, try to get you to participate in ungodly activities and seek to pressure you to make poor life choices. Ask God for help and also seek out Christian mentors and friends for support.

A prayer for you...

As _____ goes through his day, help him to set boundaries with time management. Also, help him to notice the people who influence his life. Please give him wisdom to set boundaries with those who are toxic and unhealthy. Please provide some strong support in the form of godly friends and Christian role models that can come along side him and affirm him as he sets these boundaries.

Examples of healthy boundaries...

Day 22

Wisdom Beyond Measure

Wisdom:

The right use or exercise of knowledge; the choice of laudable ends, and of the best means to accomplish them

The Bible Says...

Therefore be careful how you walk, not as unwise men but as wise, making the most of your time, because the days are evil. So then do not be foolish, but understand what the will of the Lord is.
EPHESIANS 5:15-17

Seeking God's will and direction is the wisest choice you can make. With his guidance, you can not go wrong.

Discretion will guard you, understanding will watch over you...
PROVERBS 2:11

Wisdom from the Bible can help you make the right choices which can prevent some terrible and life altering mistakes.

Listen to counsel...that you may be wise the rest of your days.
PROVERBS 19:20

Listening to godly advice is so beneficial. It can help you discern and guide you toward making the best decision.

Who among you is wise and understanding? Let him show by his good behavior his deeds in the gentleness of wisdom...But the wisdom from Heaven is first pure, then peaceable, gentle, reasonable, full of mercy and good fruits, unwavering, without hypocrisy.
JAMES 3:13-17

Some may consider a lot of academic knowledge as wisdom, but true wisdom is following what God wants. By living in such a way that is gentle, merciful, peaceful, strong in faith and genuine, you are pleasing God and being wise.

I will instruct you and teach you in the way which you should go; I will counsel you with My eye upon you.
PSALM 32:8

if any of you lacks wisdom, you should ask God, who gives generously to all without finding fault, and it will be given to you...
JAMES 1:5

When you are uncertain about anything, seek God and he will counsel you and show you what to do. He will be faithful in this.

Set up for yourself road marks, place for yourself guideposts; direct your mind to the highway, the way by which you went...
JEREMIAH 31:21

Learning from mistakes and taking note of what can be changed is very wise.

A prayer for you...

Lord, please give _____ your version of wisdom found in the Bible. Help him to seek you for clarity and to know that he can trust you for direction and guidance. Also, please bring wise people into his life and let him be open to godly advice.

I'm praying God will give you wisdom...

Day 23

A Godly Leader

Leader:

A LEADER; A GUIDE; ONE CONDUCTS- WHO GOES BEFORE OR ACCOMPANIES, AND SHOWS THE WAY.

The Bible says...

I can do all things through Him who strengthens me.
PHILIPPIANS 4:13

Sometimes leading and taking initiative can be difficult. But, God can give courage and resolve as needed for those to do the leadership tasks he has called them to do. He can help people to spiritually stretch, get out of their comfort zone and lead with his strength.

Let us hold fast the confession of our hope without wavering, for He who promised is faithful...
HEBREWS 10:23

A godly man prioritizes going to church and serving others. He loves his other people well and teaches them Biblical truths through his words and actions. He is faithful and unwaivering in his commitment to God.

Let no one look down on your youthfulness, but rather in speech, conduct, love, faith and purity, show yourself an example of those who believe.
1 TIMOTHY 4:12

A godly leader has committed his life to the Lord. His speech is edifying, his love for others is evident, his faith is strong and his life is morally sound.

...walk in a manner worthy of the calling with which you have been called, with all humility and gentleness, with patience, [bearing with one another] in love, being diligent to preserve the unity of the Spirit in the bond of peace.

EPHESIANS 4:1-3

Humility, patience, gentleness, love and an attitude of peace are all qualities that create an excellent leader. Also, one of the most important responsibilities God has for a godly leader is to treat his family well. God wants the man to be a spiritual leader in his home, to value and treasure his future wife, just like Jesus values and cares for us. With God's help, these character traits can develop.

A prayer for you...

Lord, please fill _____ with your Spirit and presence so that he will be a godly leader and a person of gentleness, humility, love, honor and peace. Look upon him with favor and let him know he is valuable to you. As he seeks your guidance, show him how to be a good leader.

Leadership qualities I see in you...

Day 24

Talents and Abilities

Talent:

NATURAL GIFT OR ENDOWMENT

The Bible says...

Do you see a man skilled in his work? He will stand before kings; He will not stand before obscure men.

Proverbs 22:29

Doing work well, no matter how big or small the task, will leave you with a good reputation that will be valued.

Whether, then, you eat or drink or whatever you do, do all to the glory of God...

PROVERBS 31:24

All that we do comes from God. He made you and has given you specific talents and abilities, so it is fitting to honor and thank him.

And there are varieties of ministries, and the same Lord. There are varieties of effects, but the same God who works all things in all persons.

1 CORINTHIANS 12:5-6

Your gifts are part of a bigger picture. God has given everyone abilities. For those who are committed to the Lord, God uses those gifts in particular ways to encourage others and glorify him.

As each one has received a special gift, employ it in serving one another as good stewards of the manifold grace of God.
1 PETER 4:10

You have special gifts that are specific to you. God wants you to use your talents to bless other people.

And He [Christ] gave some as apostles, and some as prophets, and some as evangelists, and some as pastors and teachers, for the equipping of the saints for the work of service, to the building up of the body of Christ…
EPHESIANS 4:11-12

God has a purpose for your life. You may not know what it is yet, but if you trust him, he will show you. Along with this, he has some unique tasks he wants you to do with the talents and abilities he has given you.

A prayer for you…

Thank you Jesus for the talents that you have given _____. Please Lord, help him to use these special abilities to honor you and to serve others. Let him be a good steward of what you have gifted. As he grows closer to you, help him to find out more about his unique spiritual gifts. Let him use those in a way to bring people closer to you and to influence others for Christ.

Some talents I see in you...

Day 25

A Courageous Spirit

Courage:

BRAVERY; INTREPIDITY; THAT QUALITY OF MIND WHICH ENABLES MEN TO ENCOUNTER DANGER AND DIFFICULTIES WITH FIRMNESS, OR WITHOUT FEAR OR DEPRESSION OF SPIRITS; VALOR; BOLDNESS; RESOLUTION

The Bible says...

Have I not commanded you? Be strong and courageous! Do not tremble or be dismayed, for the LORD your God is with you wherever you go.
JOSHUA 1:9

Circumstances may make you feel fearful, but God is with you in all situations and everywhere you go. He is holding your hand and guiding you.

Therefore let us draw near with confidence to the throne of grace, so that we may receive mercy and find grace to help in time of need.
HEBREWS 4:16

When you need help, there is no better helper than Jesus. Because of God's grace and forgiveness, you can talk to God with boldness and confidence knowing that he is merciful and will listen.

He Himself has said, "I will never desert you, nor will I ever forsake you," so that we confidently say, "The Lord is my helper, I will not be afraid. What will man do to me?"
HEBREWS 13:6

Others may desert you, but God will never leave you. Your Creator is your helper. You don't have to be afraid of anyone or anything when he is with you.

The wicked flee when no one is pursuing, but the righteous are bold as a lion.
PROVERBS 28:1

We can be confident that when we do what is right, there is nothing to hide. We can be bold in our faith because of our strength in God.

"For I know the plans that I have for you," declares the LORD, "plans for welfare and not for calamity to give you a future and a hope. Then you will call upon Me and come and pray to Me, and I will listen to you. You will seek Me and find Me when you search for Me with all your heart."
JEREMIAH 29:11-13

God has good plans for you. He has a future for you. With him there is hope, here on Earth and also for eternity. You can take courage knowing that God is listening to you and is with you.

A prayer for you...

Please give _____ the courage to approach you without fear or hesitancy. Show him that in Christ he can be courageous, confident, fearless and secure. Help him to be able to share his needs and problems with you Father. Strengthen him in those situations when he may be scared. Protect and watch over him. Guard his life. Let him not lose heart, but know that your strong presence is beside him to give him strength and courage.

Praying that God will give you courage in these specific areas...

God is always with you...

What a healthy church looks like...

A few more thoughts to share...

The Lord bless _____ and keep you;
The Lord make His face shine on you,
and be gracious to you;
The Lord lift up His countenance on you,
And give you peace.

Numbers 6:24-26

Purpose and Hope with God as Your Captain: 25 Days of Biblical Truths With My Prayers and Notes of Encouragement for You- An Amazing Young Man

ISBN: 978-1-7344708-7-1

© 2020 by Rebekah Tague

Scripture quotations taken from the New American Standard Bible® (NASB), Copyright © 1960, 1962, 1963, 1968, 1971, 1972, 1973, 1975, 1977, 1995 by The Lockman Foundation

Used by permission. www.Lockman.org

Dictionary quotations taken from: Webster, Noah. An American Dictionary of the English Language : Intended to Exhibit, I. The Origin, Affinities and Primary Signification of English Words, As Far As They Have Been Ascertained; II. the Genuine Orthography and Pronunciation of Words, According to General. S. Converse, Printed by Hezekiah Howe, 1828.

Copyright: Public Domain

All Hymns Copyright: Public Domain

All photography is the property of Rebekah Tague

Questions? Comments? Please write to prayerlegacybooks@gmail.com

This book is dedicated my best friend, my husband. Thank you for being so supportive and encouraging during this writing process and always. You are such a wonderful person. You truly are my "Gift from God".

Check out these other titles...

A Pregnancy Devotional- I'm Praying for You: 40 Weeks of Scripture, Prayer and Reflection for Your Developing Baby- ISBN 978-0-692-05283-9

A Grandparent's Devotional- I'm Praying for You: 40 Weeks of Scripture, Prayer and Reflection for Your Developing Grandbaby- ISBN 978-1-7344708-5-7

A Grandparent's Devotional- Close to My Heart: 40 Weeks of Scripture, Prayer and Reflection for Your Grandchild- ISBN 978-1-7344708-1-9

Son, You are Esteemed and Loved: 40 Weeks of Scripture, Prayer and Reflection for My Incredible Son- ISBN 978-1-7344708-4-0

Daughter, You are Treasured and Loved: 40 Weeks of Scripture, Prayer and Reflection for My Cherished Daughter- ISBN 978-1-7344708-3-3

For a child/teen in foster care or a child/young adult being mentored...

Praying You are Rooted and Growing: 25 Days of Biblical Truths with My Prayers and Notes of Encouragement for You- An Amazing Young Woman

ISBN 978-1-7344708-6-4

Sharing the good news and gospel of Jesus Christ...

In Dark Uncertainty, Know the Light of the World: 13 Days of Biblical Truths of the Christian Faith, with My Prayers and Notes of Encouragement for You

ISBN 978-1-7344708-8-8

www.ingramcontent.com/pod-product-compliance
Lightning Source LLC
Chambersburg PA
CBHW042025100526
44587CB00029B/4303